The Jewish Value of Giving

Foreword

Philanthropy is a magnificent force for good, transforming both recipient and donor.

Its power today is unprecedented. Its scale and societal reach continue to expand faster than ever. And, as has been the case throughout history, its practice is led disproportionately by members of our Jewish faith.

Like everything about Jews and Judaism, there is a uniquely *Jewish* approach to philanthropy. It is best known by its Hebrew name, *tzedakah*. The Greek *philanthrōpía* means love of mankind—a noble emotion, to be sure. *Tzedakah*, by contrast, is rooted in the term *tzedek*, which means justice. This stark distinction and its practical implications are skillfully documented in the following pages.

As Jews, we look back before moving forward. The further we look into the astonishing history of *tzedakah*—stretching, as it does, back across every era of our history—and the more carefully we examine the wealth of Jewish literature on the topic, the deeper and more impactful will be our experience.

Tzedakah lies not only in the heart of the Jew, but at the heart of Judaism. It springs not from whim or want, but from an illuminating set of consistent guidelines and a hierarchy of priorities. It is informed by profoundly inspiring messages from the Torah and its sages that turn charity into a rewarding way of life and a transformative way of serving our Creator, to the greater benefit of our people and of society at large.

This booklet presents an informative sampling of Judaism's essential perspectives on and guidelines for philanthropy. After reading it, one cannot but be motivated toward an increased appreciation of *tzedakah*, most especially in support of Jewish causes. And one cannot but marvel at the contributions of the Torah and its people to the betterment of civilization.

Ancient golden Byzantine coins.

ב"ה

Contents

1.	Why Give?	5
2.	What Are the Benefits of Giving?	13
3.	How Much to Give?	21
4.	When Giving Is Hard	29
5.	Priorities in Giving	37
6.	Must My Motive Be Pure?	45
7.	Should My Gift Be Publicized?	51
8.	A History of Jewish Giving	57
9.	Instilling the Value of *Tzedakah*	63
10.	The Time Is Now	73

1. Why Give?

WHY GIVE?

The Jewish nation was born through acts of charity. Abraham offered free meals to weary travelers for the sake of spreading kindness. He was so very charitable that God promised to bring forth a unique nation from Abraham—a people naturally disposed to caring and empathy, to the point that the Talmud considers this trait an identifying feature of a Jew. Ours is a nation that cannot live simply to sustain itself. We consider life meaningless without the opportunity to advance worthy causes.

In the universal view of charity, kind benefactors take a loss to benefit others. The Torah insists on the reverse: God withholds wealth from some to give benefactors the opportunity to come to their aid. Seen through this lens, a pauper is the ultimate donor, and a philanthropist the ultimate recipient. This is why the Torah declares that a benefactor's money is not his own; God provided it to him only so that he use it to care for the needy. Hence, the Torah refers to this act as justice (*tzedakah*), underscoring by its very name that it is an obligation and simply the just thing to do. Given the chance to assist, a Jewish donor is genuinely grateful for the opportunity.

According to Jewish mysticism, God designed a world that requires constant acts of kindness, because charity is the strongest tool for remodeling the universe into a home for God. Earnings are the product of planning, creativity, effort, investment, and infrastructure—and with a single act of charity, all this is spiritually elevated and connected to the Divine purpose of bringing Heaven down to earth.

Sources: Genesis 21:33; Talmud, Sotah 10b; *Mishneh Torah,* Laws of Gifts to the Poor 10:1; Talmud, Yevamot 79a; Rabbi Samson Raphael Hirsch, Deuteronomy 15:7; *Arbaah Turim, Yoreh De'ah* 247; *Tanchuma, Mishpatim* 9; *Likutei Sichot* 2:410; *Tanya,* ch. 37.

Donation bowl for poor brides from the Schiffschul synagogue; main inscription reads (tr.), "Great is charity to wed poor brides." Vienna, 1910.

SUPPORTING TEXTS

A JEWISH TRAIT
Maimonides, *Mishneh Torah*, Laws of Gifts to the Poor 10:1

We are obligated to be careful with regard to the mitzvah of charity to a greater extent than all other commandments, because charity is an identifying trait of a descendant of our patriarch Abraham, as it says (Genesis 18:19), "I love Abraham because he instructs his children that they should perform *tzedakah*...."

FOR THE PURPOSE OF PROVIDING
Midrash, *Tanchuma*, Mishpatim 9

King David exclaimed to God, "Master of the Universe!... Establish equity in Your world by making rich and poor equal!"
God replied, "If such were the case, 'Who would preserve kindness and truth?' (Psalms 61:8). If all were rich or all were poor, who would be able to perform acts of kindness?"

UNRIVALED SPIRITUAL ELEVATION
Rabbi Shne'ur Zalman of Liadi, *Tanya*, ch. 37

Our sages greatly extolled the virtue of charity, declaring it equal to all the other *mitzvot* combined (Talmud, Bava Batra 9a).... This is because charity is at the core of all the *mitzvot* and surpasses them all. The purpose of all *mitzvot* is to elevate our life force to God... and you will find no other mitzvah in which the life force is engaged to the same extent as in the mitzvah of charity. For in all other *mitzvot*, only one of our faculties is invested in the mitzvah, and only while the mitzvah is being performed. In the case of charity, however, we give from the proceeds of our hard work, and all of our life force is invested in our work.... Thus, when we give the proceeds of our work to charity, our entire life force is elevated to God....

This is why the Talmud states that charity hastens the Redemption (Bava Batra 10a). For with one act of charity, one elevates much more of the life force than is elevated through the performance of many other *mitzvot* combined.

YOUR WEALTH IS GOD'S DEPOSIT
Rabbi Yaakov Ben Asher, *Arbaah Turim, Yoreh De'ah* 247

It is an affirmative commandment of the Torah to give *tzedakah* according to one's means. A person must be extremely vigilant with this mitzvah, more so than with any other affirmative commandment.... We should take to heart the following consideration: just as we ask God to facilitate a livelihood for us, and just as we ask that He listen to our pleadings, so do we need to listen to the pleadings of those who need charity....

Let not evil counsel arise in your heart that says, "How can I reduce my own wealth by giving it away to the poor?" *Know that the wealth is not yours*; it is only a deposit given on condition that you use it as the Depositor desires, giving a portion of it to the poor.

NATURALLY GENEROUS
Rabbi Samson Raphael Hirsch, Deuteronomy 15:7

Regarding the mitzvah of charity, the verse states, "Do not harden your heart and do not close your hand." The implication of this verse is that the Jewish heart is naturally inclined toward kindness and generosity. It is possible to crush these feelings by cold calculations and a love for money, but this, the verse tells us, we must overcome.

Woman, Child and Begging Bowl, Seated Jewish man with Instrument, *Josef Süss, 1920*

Sir Moses Montefiore on the cover of Harper's Weekly, *October 20, 1883. (Harvard University Press)*

STORY Sir Moses Montefiore was an outstanding Anglo-Jewish philanthropist of the nineteenth century, and the first Jew to attain high office in the City of London. On his one hundredth birthday, *The London Times* devoted editorials to his praise, noting that "he had shown that fervent Judaism and patriotic citizenship are absolutely consistent with one another."

He was asked, "Sir Moses, what are you worth?" Moses thought for a while and named a figure far too small for an international merchant prince of his magnitude.

"But surely," pressed his astonished interviewer, "your wealth must be much more than that!"

Sir Moses gently replied, "You didn't ask me how much I own. You asked me how much I am worth. So I calculated how much I have given to charity this year.

"You see," he explained, "we are only worth what we are willing to share with others."

Central field of 18th-century embroidered Torah mantle; the full inscription, part of which is visible below, reads: (tr.), "Donated by Yokev ben Ziskind, head of the Bohemian Landesjudenschaft, and his wife Sarl bat Iserl." (Jewish Museum in Prague)

2. What Are the Benefits of Giving?

Benefits

Give and you shall prosper, declares Judaism about the mitzvah (commandment) of *tzedakah* (charity). As much as the benefactor helps the recipient, the recipient helps the benefactor even more.

At first blush this seems counterintuitive. Yet this surprising claim is reaffirmed throughout the Jewish canon: *Tzedakah* is the proverbial candle that can kindle a thousand others; it is a well that never runs dry. Not only does it not diminish one's wealth, but God pledges that sharing with others actually *increases* a donor's wealth. "Set aside a tenth of your produce," the Torah instructs the Jewish farmer, "so that you may become wealthy."[1] Unlike other *mitzvot*, the reward for which is reserved for the hereafter, God promises to repay *tzedakah* in the here-and-now.

But money isn't everything. Giving charity, of course, produces other important positive outcomes, many of which have been demonstrated empirically. For example, better health and higher levels of happiness have been associated with charitable giving. Indeed, researchers have discovered that a leading predictor of

---

1. Deuteronomy 14:22; Talmud, Taanit 9a.

happiness is not one's wealth or personal spending, but rather *how much one spends on others.*

We are conditioned to think of our money as a fixed pie: parting with some of it implies that we are left with less. With *tzedakah*, however, God blows the lid off that belief system by showing His hand and directly intervening in the natural order.

The great Rabbi Akiva once told his daughter, "Charity delivers from death"[2]—literally so, to be sure, but also figuratively—offering us a taste of transcendence, a glimpse of immortality.

Sources: *Ruth Rabah* 5:9; *Shemot Rabah, Tetsaveh* 36; The Lubavitcher Rebbe, English letter, July 30, 1973; Talmud, Taanit 9a; David Pelcovitz, *Life in the Balance* (New York: Shaar Press, 2014), pp. 67–68; Elizabeth W. Dunn, et al., "Spending Money on Others Promotes Happiness," *Science*, 319 (5870), March 21, 2008, pp. 1687–1688.

---

2. Talmud, Shabbat 156b.

SUPPORTING TEXTS

THE RECIPIENT BENEFITS THE BENEFACTOR
Midrash, *Ruth Rabah* 5:9

As much as the benefactor helps the recipient, the recipient helps the benefactor even more.

NO DIMINUTION
Midrash, *Shemot Rabah*, Tetsaveh 36

What is the meaning of the verse, "A mitzvah is a candle" (Proverbs 6:23)?... It often happens that people wish to perform a mitzvah but their evil inclination persuades them not to. It tells them that they will lose money or deprive their children of future benefits. The good inclination then tells them that they *should* perform the mitzvah, explaining, "See, the Torah compares a mitzvah to a candle. Once a candle is lit, it can ignite a thousand other candles and its own light will remain in its original state, undiminished. Similarly, when you perform a mitzvah, nothing will be diminished from your possessions."

SO THAT YOU WILL BECOME WEALTHY
Talmud, Taanit 9a

"A tithe shall you tithe [*aser te'aser*]" (Deuteronomy 14:22). [The double expression used in this commandment introduces a deeper meaning, so that it can also be understood as Divine advice,] "Give the tithe [*aser*] in order that you will become wealthy [*titasher*]."
Rabbi Yochanan once encountered the young son of Reish Lakish. He said to the boy, "Recite for me a verse that you studied today."
The boy responded, "A tithe shall you tithe," and asked Rabbi Yochanan to explain the purpose of the double expression.
Rabbi Yochanan told him, "Take a tithe so that you will become wealthy."
The boy exclaimed to Rabbi Yochanan, "How do you know that this is so?"
Rabbi Yochanan told him, "Go and test it!"
The boy insisted, "But are we permitted to test God? Is it not written, 'You shall not test God' (Deuteronomy 6:16)?"
Rabbi Yochanan responded by citing Rabbi Hoshaya, "It is prohibited to test God, except in the case of tithes, as it is stated, 'Bring the whole tithe into the storeroom . . . and test Me now by this, says God, if I will not open for you the windows of Heaven, and pour out for you a blessing that there shall be more than what is sufficient' (Malachi 3:10)."

CHARITY LEADS TO
HAPPINESS

Elizabeth W. Dunn, et al. "Spending Money on Others Promotes Happiness," *Science*, 319:5870 (March 21, 2008), pp. 1687–1688

A large body of research has demonstrated that income has a . . . surprisingly weak, effect on happiness . . . particularly once basic needs are met. . . .

We asked a nationally representative sample of 632 Americans (55% female) to rate their general happiness, to report their annual income, and to estimate how much they spent in a typical month on (i) bills/expenses, (ii) gifts for themselves, (iii) gifts for others, and (iv) donations to charity. The first two categories were summed to create an index of personal spending, and the latter two categories were summed to create an index of pro-social spending. Entering the personal and pro-social spending indices simultaneously into a regression predicting general happiness revealed that personal spending was unrelated to happiness, but higher pro-social spending was associated with significantly greater happiness. . . .

We tested . . . the happiness of 16 employees before and after they received a profit-sharing bonus from their company. . . . Employees who devoted more of their bonus to pro-social spending experienced greater happiness after receiving the bonus, and the manner in which they spent that bonus was a more important predictor of their happiness than the size of the bonus itself. . . .

Our findings suggest that very minor alterations in spending allocations—as little as $5 in our final study—may be sufficient to produce nontrivial gains in happiness on a given day. Why, then, don't people make these small changes? . . . Tests revealed that participants were doubly wrong about the impact of money on happiness: we found that a significant majority thought that personal spending would make them happier than pro-social spending.

REPORTED HAPPINESS

Average
Those who give charity +43%

Source: Social Capital Community Benchmark Survey (Harvard, 2000)

Jewish Cart *(in Shtetl). Edward Gurevich, 2012, oil painting.*

STORY Reb Mordechai Rivkin, together with Reb Abba Pliskin, used to raise money for an underground yeshiva in Communist Russia. They approached a previous donor, who said that he could not give that year because business was tough.

Reb Abba answered with the following story: There was once a man who would travel to the fair every year to buy merchandise for his small-town store. Once, he was traveling home with his goods when it started raining, and the wagon got stuck in the mud. The wagon driver said that they needed to lighten the load, and suggested they throw off some of the merchandise. "I can't afford to lose my merchandise," the businessman answered, "so how about we remove the wagon's heavy wooden wheels to lighten the load?..."

Tzedakah is no more a luxury than are wheels of a wagon, Reb Abba explained. Rather, acts of *tzedakah* are the wheels that keep your business turning.

19th-century bimah cover; inscription reads (tr.), "Donated from the funds of the burial society." (Jewish Museum in Prague)

# 3. How Much to Give?

HOW MUCH?

The first recorded act of tithing, giving away a tenth of income or agricultural output, occurred some 3700 years ago, when the forefather of the Jewish nation, Abraham, gave "a tithe from all" he owned to Malchizedek, "a priest to the Most High God."[1] This tradition was passed down through Abraham's family; his grandson Jacob vowed to God that "from everything that You give me, I will surely tithe to You."[2]

At Mount Sinai, God established this ancient practice as Torah law for all future generations of Jews, primarily in the form of agricultural and animal tithes from produce and livestock. Jewish farmers separated two annual tithes before using the rest of their produce as they saw fit. This gave rise to the Jewish tradition of donating, at minimum, one-tenth of one's income to the needy, to the support of Torah institutions, or to mitzvah causes. This disciplined regimen of donation is known as *maaser*, "a tenth," and it has been the standard for Jewish giving for millennia. Jewish tradition also teaches that it is particularly laudatory if one is able to contribute two annual tithes (twenty percent) annually, thereby mirroring the double tithe from the biblical period.

---

1. Genesis 14:20.
2. Genesis 28:22.

Similar to taxes imposed by governments, several stipulations and laws govern the obligation of *maaser*. An example is the extent to which one may deduct certain expenses from income before calculating the amount due as *maaser*. A critical difference between taxes and tithes is that taxes are often resented and require human enforcement, whereas *maaser* is a duty and privilege that has been observed throughout the ages, and is followed today by Jews worldwide, out of wholehearted commitment to the Creator of the universe.

Sources: Leviticus 27:32; Deuteronomy 14:22, 14:29 with Rashi ad loc.; *Tosafot*, Taanit 9a; Shulchan Aruch, *Yoreh De'ah* 249:1, 4; *Tzedakah Umishpat* 5:8; "*Maaser Kesafim* and the Development of the Tax Law," *Florida Tax Review* 8:1 (2007).

Illustration from the Harrison Miscellany: Poems and Prayers for Weddings and Other Occasions, gouache on parchment, Corfu, c. 1720. (The Braginsky Collection)

SUPPORTING TEXTS

THE BIBLICAL COMMAND TO TITHE
Deuteronomy 14:22

You shall tithe all the crop that the field gives forth, year by year.

TITHING FROM ALL MONETARY GAINS
Tosafot, Taanit 9a

How can we infer that it applies not only to grain but also to interest, business gains, and all other forms of profit? Because the verse says, "You shall tithe all the crop," when it could have plainly said, "You shall tithe the crop." This [superfluous and more inclusive word] teaches us to tithe interest, business gains, and all other profits.

SOURCE OF ONE FIFTH
Rabbi Betzalel Ashkenazi, Ketubot 50a

The Jerusalem Talmud states that the sages enacted at Usha that Jews ought to dispense a fifth of their income for the mitzvah.... The basis for this seems to be the Torah's obligation that the Jewish farmer give two annual tithes. The first tithe went to a Levite, and, depending on the year, the second tithe was either given to the poor or brought to Jerusalem to be enjoyed there by the owner [who would also share it with others].

CREATING A TITHING ACCOUNT
Rabbi Yeshayah HaLevi Horowitz, Shenei Luchot Haberit, Tractate Chulin

One should designate a special place to store one's tithing funds, distributing from it to worthy causes.

WHICH EXPENSES MAY BE EXCLUDED
Rabbi Yaakov Yeshaya Blau, Tzedakah Umishpat 5:8

One should not deduct family expenses from one's profit. Halachic experts, however, maintain that one can deduct business expenses. One tithes from the net profit minus business expenses.

SECULAR TAX LAWS VS. THE TORAH'S TITHING LAWS
Adam Chodorow, "Maaser Kesafim and the Development of the Tax Law," Florida Tax Review 8:1 (2007), p. 195

One of the key differences between the Federal tax system and *maaser kesafim* is the need for enforcement. Compliance with the tithing laws is left to the individual, who generally views it as a sacred obligation. God acts as the arbiter over whether the individual properly fulfilled his obligation. Accordingly, the practice lacks any human audit function or enforcement mechanisms. The lack of enforcement concerns allowed the rabbis to develop rules that accurately reflect theoretical notions of income, but which would be largely unworkable if they had to be administered. In contrast, the government must enforce the tax laws against a population that largely resents the obligation and constantly seeks ways to avoid it. Thus, the tax laws must take into account compliance norms, the resources available to administer the laws, and the government's ability to evaluate and adjudicate taxpayer claims in a fair and consistent manner.

PERCENTAGES AND MINIMUMS
Rabbis Yosef Caro and Moshe Isserlis, Shulchan Aruch, *Yoreh De'ah* **249:1, 4**

It is forbidden to turn away a *tzedakah* request empty-handed. Even the smallest amount is considered giving, as it says (Psalms 74:21), "Do not let the oppressed retreat disgraced."

THREE TIERS OF GIVING
RABBIS YOSEF CARO AND MOSHE ISSERLIS, SHULCHAN ARUCH, *YOREH DE'AH* 249:1

1	If you can afford it, provide recipients with all of their needs.	"You shall surely open your hand and provide sufficiently for their needs that they are lacking" (Deuteronomy 15:8).
2	If you cannot do so, give up to twenty percent of your income. This is the ideal way of performing the mitzvah.	"This is rooted in the norm during Temple times, when Jews would donate two tithes each year" (Rabbi Meir Hameili, cited in *Shitah Mikubetset*, Ketubot 50).
3	If you cannot do so, give ten percent of your income. This is the ordinary way of doing this mitzvah; giving less is miserly.	"Then Abram gave a tenth of everything" (Genesis 14:20). "Jacob made a vow saying . . . 'And of all that You give me I will give to you a tenth'" (Genesis 28:20–22).

Eight Levels of *Tzedakah* Giving
Maimonides, *Mishneh Torah*, Laws of Gifts to the Poor 10:7–14

Jewish Eight Levels of Tzedaka (detail). Sharon Feldstein, mixed media on canvas.

1	Providing a loan, job, or partnership, so that the recipient no longer needs charity
2	The benefactor and recipient do not know each other's identity.
3	The benefactor knows the recipient, but the recipient does not know the benefactor.
4	The recipient knows the benefactor, but the benefactor does not know the recipient.
5	Giving before being asked
6	Giving the correct amount upon request
7	Giving less than what one could be giving, but with a smile
8	Giving unhappily

Triptych (detail, from leftmost of three panels),
Benjamin Senior Godines, c.1680, oil painting.
(Jewish Museum, London)

4. When Giving Is Hard

WHEN IT'S HARD

Money is hard to part with. People may consider their income insufficient to justify donations to worthy causes.

Ironically, it is precisely when "I can't" is the instinctive response that *tzedakah* is most beneficial. It demands a courageous demonstration of faith in God's intimate control over human affairs, a trust that is deeply treasured by God, in return for which He commands His blessings to increase our earnings.

Judaism accepts payment plans. For example, when it is difficult to donate *maaser*, a tenth of one's earnings, one may make a partial donation, and leave the balance as a debt to be paid as soon as it becomes feasible.

But is one's income really insufficient? The Torah associates charity with judgment, because it is human nature to permit ourselves luxuries while convincing ourselves that we cannot afford to support important Jewish institutions. Jews must, therefore, judge themselves with honest scrutiny to avoid self-deception. It takes humility to spend less on indulgences for the sake of increasing assistance to worthy causes, and this is precisely what makes one a better person in the eyes of God and man.

The difficulty to give is sometimes not due to financial hardship or indulgences but to the fact that it is simply not easy to part with one's money. The Torah gives us a timeless tithing tip: First focus on what you have. Count your coins carefully, so you can appreciate what blessings God has allowed you to earn and to spend as you wish. You will then be able to turn your attention to the percentage that God asks you to donate with a full and grateful heart.

Sources: Talmud, Gitin 7a; *Kedushat Levi, Pirushei Agadot; Igrot Kodesh* 17:262, 27:91; Genesis 21:33; *Torat Chayim, Shemot* 1:173d–174a; Talmud, Bechorot 58b; *Ateret Chaim* (Halberstam) 2:31–32.

Donation advertiser, Austria, c. 1850.
(Jewish Museum Vienna)

SUPPORTING TEXTS

GIVE WHEN FINANCES ARE LIMITED
Talmud, Gitin 7a

If you see that your sustenance is limited, use it for charity—all the more so when it is plentiful.

CONNECT TO THE SOURCE OF BLESSING
Rabbi Levi Yitschak of Berditchev, Kedushat Levi, Pirushei Agadot

The Talmud states that those whose assets are dwindling should increase their charitable giving. But why specifically this mitzvah? The answer is that the Torah is hereby teaching us the proper way to live our lives.

Placing trust in a worldly entity implies that something other than God maintains a degree of control. . . . Instead, we place our trust in God alone and recognize that only He exerts any control. We thus connect to God, the source of life, and we will find blessings of plenty in all our affairs.

The sages therefore advise those whose assets are dwindling to give charity. Disbursing charity under such conditions demonstrates absolute belief and trust in God. . . . This trust will bring blessing and success to all of their affairs and cause their holdings to multiply.

FORGO LUXURY TO INCREASE CHARITY
Rabbi Dovber of Lubavitch, Torat Chayim, Shemot 1:173d–174a

When people contemplate and empathize with the plight of those in need, they will certainly be meticulous to exercise strict judgment on themselves . . . not to spend their money on luxuries but only on the minimum that they need for themselves and their families. . . . One who reduces spending on luxuries and instead allocates this money to *tzedakah* is called a *ba'al tzedakah*—a charitable person.

Thus, a crucial element of *tzedakah* is contingent on *mishpat*—self-judgment—which is why these two values are linked in Genesis 18:19. People ought to evaluate their own spending and to suffice only with what is really needed. . . . *Tzedakah* and *mishpat*—judgment—are thus intertwined.

Often, indulging in luxury emerges from feelings of haughtiness. . . . Humble people evaluate their needs; they choose to live with less and allocate the money that they would have spent on luxuries to revive the lives of the downtrodden and to support sacred mitzvah causes.

COUNT YOUR BLESSINGS
BEFORE DONATING

Rabbi Mordechai Dov Twerski of Hornosteipel, cited in *Ateret Chayim* (Halberstam), 2:31–32

The Talmud states (Bechorot 58b), "How does one tithe animals? The owner brings them into a pen and makes a small opening. The owner then stands by the opening, and as the animals emerge, he counts, 'One, two, three,' etc. When the tenth animal emerges, the owner declares, 'This is the tithe.'" The Talmud continues with the stipulation that one who owns one hundred animals, for example, is not allowed to simply designate any ten for tithing; rather, the owner must count in this specific way.

The importance of following this specific procedure is due to the concern that were we to approach a flock in which we heavily invested and give away a tenth all at once, our compliance may be with a heavy heart or a grudging attitude. God wanted to enable us to observe this commandment with love and a positive attitude. He therefore commanded that we tithe in the specific manner outlined above. When we count the first animal and realize that it will be completely for us, and the same with the second animal, etc., and the same with the eighth and ninth animals, we come to better appreciate the great blessings that God has given us. Suddenly, the giving away of one animal is less daunting, and we can part with it with a happy heart.

This insight can prove helpful in overcoming the inner emotional challenge we often face in giving *tzedakah*. If we focus on the income with which we have been blessed, and not simply on what we are giving away, we will be better equipped to follow the Torah's command.

Pen and ink illustration found in an 18th-century kabbalistic prayer book. (The British Library)

Pen and ink illustration found in an 18th-century kabbalistic prayer book. (The British Library)

STORY Two sages were sent to raise funds for an important cause. Together, the two men headed to the home of a man named Barbohin. He was known as a wealthy man and had in the past donated generously. But when they approached his home they overheard a troubling conversation. The man's child was asking what food to buy for the day, and the father's response was to purchase endives, adding, "They should not be fresh. Make sure they are leftovers from yesterday and wilted so that they will be cheap."

Hearing this, the rabbis decided that the man must have lost his money, so they left, choosing to first collect from the others in the city.

After they had made their rounds, they came back to him. He asked them, "Why didn't you come to me first, as you usually do?"

"We did come to you first, but when we heard you talking to your son . . ."

He said to them, "You heard what was said between me and my son, but you don't know what is between me and God. With my own needs, I am allowed to take liberties and be stingy, but when it comes to the commandments of my Creator, I have no permission." And he arranged for them a handsome donation.
(Midrash, *Esther Rabah* 2:3; Jerusalem Talmud, Pesachim 4:9)

Advertisement (detail) for a performance by a young cantor, ten-year-old Kalmele Weitz, under the sponsorship of Tomkhe Aniyim (Supporters of the Poor), a charitable organization in Warsaw. (YIVO Institute for Jewish Research, New York)

5. Priorities in Giving

PRIORITIES

Jews score disproportionally high on the giving charts, often donating more than the obligatory *maaser*, a tenth of net income. This is natural for a nation whose religion inspired the modern concepts of charity, social responsibility, and equality. Nevertheless, many Jews remain unaware that the Torah sets forth specific guidelines for giving.

Today, an overwhelming majority of Jewish donations support a spectrum of universal causes, to the detriment of worthy Jewish causes. But the Torah envisions Jewish charity as radiating outward in concentric circles that are strongest at their epicenter.

The adage, "Charity begins at home," is actually a Divinely-mandated obligation. We are encouraged to prioritize needy relatives over local charities, and local institutions over nonlocal causes, giving larger amounts to those closer to our homes and communities. And because Jews are members of an extended family, we are particularly responsible for each other's welfare. Accordingly, Jews ought to direct their largest contributions to Jewish causes.

Equally important to feeding the hungry and assisting the needy is our obligation to support structures that benefit the Jewish community and nation at large, schools, *yeshivot*, other institutions of Jewish learning, synagogues and *mikva'ot* (Jewish ritual baths), recalling that Jews are responsible not only for their larger Jewish family's physical needs but also for a living Judaism and its miraculous continuity.

Sources: "Jews Take 5 of Top 6 Spots in Annual List of Top U.S. Givers," *Jewish Telegraphic Agency*, February 8, 2011; *Bikedushato Shel Aharon* (ed., Aharon Perlow), 1:68; Shulchan Aruch, *Yoreh De'ah* 251:3; *Aruch Hashulchan, Yoreh De'ah* 251:4; Talmud, Gitin 61a; Shulchan Aruch, *Choshen Mishpat* 163:3.

Beggars at the entrance to the Wailing Wall, *Yaakov Benor-Kalter (1897–1969), photograph, Jerusalem, 1925. (University of Pennsylvania Libraries, Philadelphia)*

SUPPORTING TEXTS

U.S. JEWS LEAD PHILANTHROPY, NOT TO JEWISH CAUSES
Jewish Telegraphic Agency, February 8, 2011

The Institute for Jewish and Communal Research has collected data showing that less than a quarter of all philanthropic dollars given by Jews go to overtly Jewish causes. . . .

This year's Philanthropy 50 had one major exception: Stephen and Nancy Grand, who ranked 39th, gave more than $20 million of their $28 million in 2010 charitable donations to the American Technion Society, which supports the Technion: Israel Institute for Technology. In June, the Grands helped the Technion finish off a 14-year, $1 billion fundraising campaign with their mammoth gift to the school, to which they also had given $10 million to create the Stephen and Nancy Grand Water Research Institute.

REQUIREMENT TO PRIORITIZE DONATIONS
Rabbi Shalom Rokeach of Belz, cited in *Bikedushato Shel Aharon* **(Aharon Perlow, ed.), 1:68**

Regarding the mitzvah of charity, the verse states (Deuteronomy 15:7), "Do not harden your heart and do not close your hand." Now, there are differing priorities when it comes to charitable giving: relatives precede the citizens of one's city, who precede those from elsewhere. When our hands are closed, all of our fingers appear more or less equal; when we open our hands, we notice the differences among them. By the same token, the verse instructs us, "Do not close your hand" when giving charity. In other words, do not fail to recognize the distinctions of priority.

HIERARCHY OF PHILANTHROPY
Rabbi Yosef Caro, Shulchan Aruch, *Yoreh De'ah* **251:3**

The poor of one's family take precedence over the poor of one's city. The poor of one's city take precedence over the poor of another city. When considering other cities, causes that assist Jews living in the Land of Israel take precedence over Jews living in the Diaspora.

GREATER GENEROSITY, NOT EXCLUSIVITY
Rabbi Yechiel Michel Epstein, *Aruch Hashulchan, Yoreh De'ah* **251:4**

Wealthy people and those of average means alike often have relatives who are needy. If donors prioritize the needy within their own families, what will happen to the needy who have no relatives? Will they die of hunger? Obviously, one must distribute funds to all, and the distinction is merely a question of quantity: one should distribute more to needy relatives than to other causes, and more to the needy citizens of the same city than to the poor of another city, and so forth.

OBLIGATION TO INCLUDE NON-JEWISH CAUSES
Talmud, Gitin 61a

We support the non-Jewish poor, visit their sick, and bury their dead—all for the sake of fostering the ways of peace.

RESPONSIBILITY OF INDIVIDUALS TO THEIR COMMUNITY
Rabbi Moshe Isserlis, Shulchan Aruch, *Choshen Mishpat* 163:3

When a city appoints teachers of the Torah for children because parents cannot afford to hire teachers on their own, the entire community must pay for the teachers, and residents must give in proportion to their means. The same applies to building a synagogue and hiring its staff. Individuals who have no personal need for particular communal institutions such as a *mikveh* or a wedding hall must nevertheless pay their share.

Priorities in Giving
Rabbi Yosef Caro, Shulchan Aruch, *Yoreh De'ah* 251:3

1	Your Family
2	Needy of Your City
3	Needy of Another City
4	Needy of Israel
5	Needy throughout the Diaspora

CONTRIBUTIONS ACROSS THE LANDSCAPE OF JEWISH CHARITY

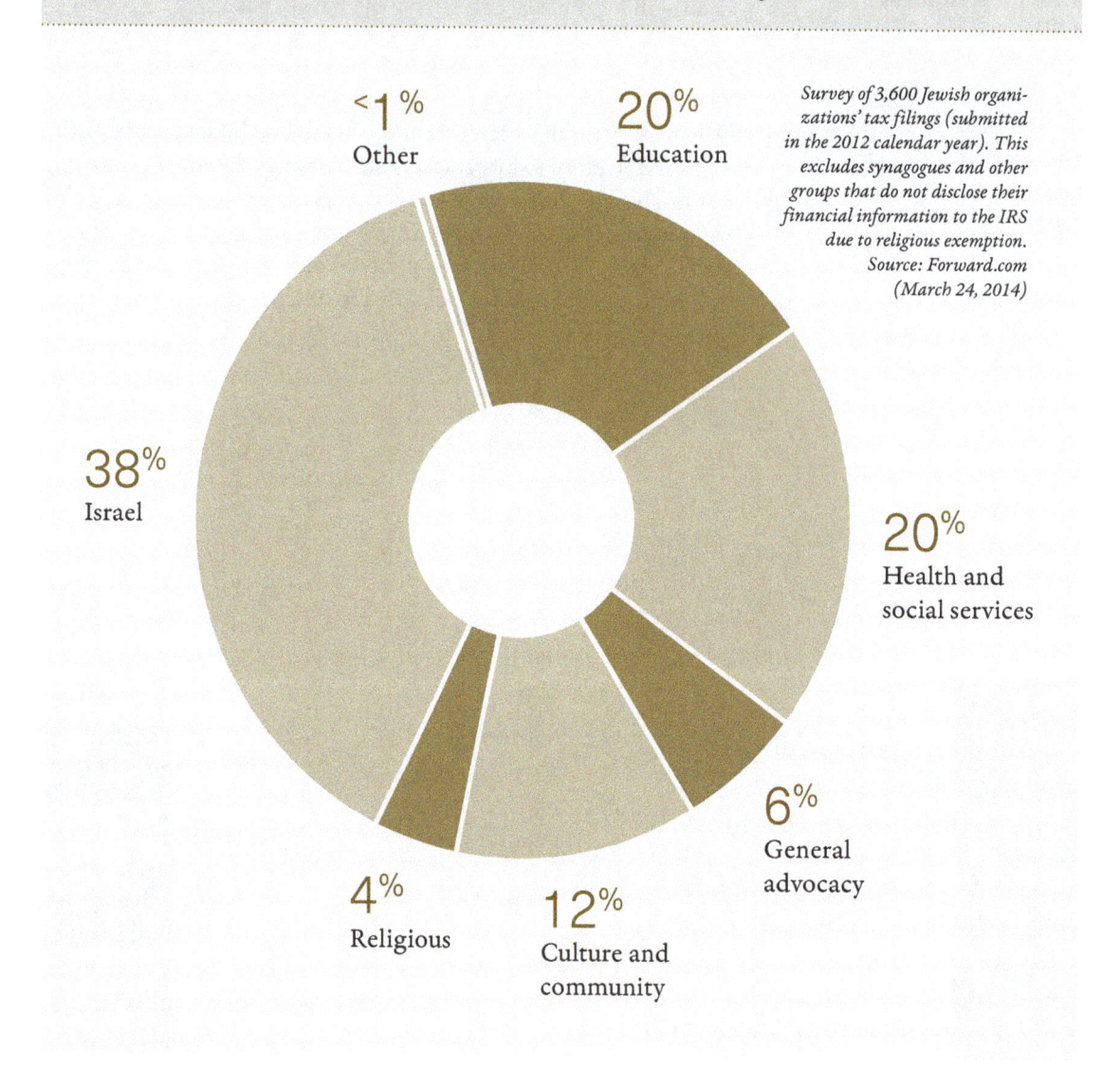

Survey of 3,600 Jewish organizations' tax filings (submitted in the 2012 calendar year). This excludes synagogues and other groups that do not disclose their financial information to the IRS due to religious exemption. Source: Forward.com (March 24, 2014)

- <1% Other
- 20% Education
- 20% Health and social services
- 6% General advocacy
- 12% Culture and community
- 4% Religious
- 38% Israel

Pen and ink illustration found in an 18th-century kabbalistic prayer book. (The British Library)

STORY There was once a wealthy couple who lost all of their money, and so the man was forced to take on various odd jobs. One day, as he was plowing a field, he met Elijah the Prophet disguised as an Arab. Elijah told the man, "You have six years of wealth coming to you. Do you want them now or at the end of your life?"

The man said to him, "Let me consult with my wife." He went to his wife and she advised that they take the money immediately. And indeed, soon thereafter, the couple's children were playing in the yard and they found there an ancient treasure.

The wife told her husband, "God has been extremely kind to us. Let's spend these six years helping others with this money." So they did exactly that.

At the end of the six years, Elijah came and told the man, "The time has come for me to take back what I gave you."

The man said, "When I accepted the money, I consulted with my wife. Now that it's time to give it back, let me consult with her again."

His wife told him, "Go and tell Elijah that if he has truly found people who will use the money better than we did, he should by all means take what he deposited with us and give it to them."

Needless to say, their blessings of wealth continued for the rest of their lives.

(*Yalkut Shimoni*, Ruth 607)

6. Must My Motive Be Pure?

MOTIVE

As a general rule, Judaism attributes significance not only to people's actions and speech, but also to their thoughts and feelings. The ideal way to perform *mitzvot*, therefore, is with pure motives. At the same time, we are encouraged to do what is right regardless of our intent, or lack thereof, in the expectation that we will eventually train ourselves to continue the same activities for the proper reasons. However, until we reach that goal, our *mitzvot* remain somewhat deficient.

Every rule has a golden exception. The chief goal of *tzedakah* is to assist others, expand institutions, increase enrollment in Torah programs, and similar practical results. It is less important that our intent be "pure," free of the expectation of spiritual reward, blessings in our affairs, or even of our own fame as philanthropists. In the realm of *tzedakah*, this ideal of purity of intent is much less important.

According to Jewish mysticism, non-altruistic giving of *tzedakah* is only the surface reality of one who supports a worthy cause. At our core, there flickers a living spark of God. Like its Creator, this Divine spark is altruistic, self-sacrificing, and longs to fulfill each mitzvah for its own sake—most especially *tzedakah*, which entails sacrificing one's earnings for the benefit of others. When we make such a donation, we are at least subconsciously propelled by an inner intent that is wholly noble and selfless.

Sources: Talmud, Bava Batra 10a; Pesachim 50b; Pesachim 8a–b; *Sifrei, Ki Tetsei* 283; *Ahavat Tzion, Drush* 10, p. 128; *Likutei Sichot* 5:248.

Stamps by Mishmeres Choylim (Guardian of the Sick), Vilna, Lithuania; Yiddish inscription translation: "Mishmeres Choylim gives the poor man a doctor at home, ice, medicine, and clinics for help." (YIVO Institute for Jewish Research, New York)

SUPPORTING TEXTS

THE VALUE OF SELFLESS PHILANTHROPY
Talmud, Bava Batra 10a

Rabban Yochanan ben Zakai once saw in a dream that his nephews were destined to lose seven hundred dinars. He encouraged them to give to charity, and they gave away seventeen dinars less than seven hundred. When Yom Kippur eve arrived, the government sent messengers who took the remaining seventeen dinars. Rabban Yochanan told them, "Do not fear; seventeen dinars is all they will take from you."

The nephews responded, "How did you know?" He replied, "I saw all of this in a dream." They asked him, "But why did you not inform us about the dream?" He explained, "I told myself that it would be better that you perform the mitzvah altruistically."

INSINCERE OBSERVANCE IS A POSITIVE FIRST STEP
Talmud, Pesachim 50b

A person should always engage in Torah and *mitzvot*, even for ulterior motives, because this will lead a person to engage in them for their own sake.

ACCIDENTAL CHARITY COUNTS
Sifrei, Ki Tetsei 283

When a person accidentally drops a coin and a pauper finds it and uses it to sustain himself, the inadvertent benefactor is credited with and rewarded for the good deed.

NON-ALTRUISTIC DONATIONS ARE ACCEPTABLE
Talmud, Pesachim 8a–b

It has been taught: If one declares, "I am giving this coin to charity so that my child shall live," or "so that I shall merit a portion in the World to Come"—this person is completely righteous.

WHY MOTIVES CANNOT MAR CHARITY
Rabbi Yechezkel Landau, cited in Ahavat Tzion, Drush 10, p. 128

If you take a *lulav*, lay *tefilin*, or wear *tsitsit* without any recognition that you are performing a mitzvah, you have accomplished nothing. These acts are not inherently valuable or helpful, other than by virtue of them being God's commands; it is the commandment alone that accords value and importance to these actions. Therefore, if you perform these acts without consciously internalizing the fact that they are commandments, you have done nothing.

On the other hand, if you give charity without considering at all that it is a mitzvah, there is nevertheless a bottom-line benefit for the recipient. To the poor, it makes no difference whether the donor gave the charity knowing it is a mitzvah or not.

If overall knowledge that one is doing a mitzvah is not needed, the imperative of not having ulterior motives is less important.

THE SOUL IS ALWAYS SELFLESS

The Lubavitcher Rebbe, *Likutei Sichot* **5:248**

The Talmud says that if one gives charity so that his child shall live . . . the giver is completely righteous. Although on a conscious level this gift results from an ulterior motive, there is also an internal reality that is marked by noble intentions, stemming from the fact that at the core, every Jew wishes to perform all of the *mitzvot*. So it is not just that the charitable act is complete; the giver, at least internally, is also complete.

Studying Bible. Leonid Afremov, palette knife modern oil painting on canvas.

STORY A wealthy Jewish innkeeper who was legendary for his hospitality and charity was once visited by a Chasidic rebbe, who stayed at his inn for several days. The innkeeper, seeing that his guest was a holy man, went to the rebbe and complained about the deep satisfaction he received from his charitable works. "I feel terrible that the good I do is driven by selfish intent. Should I put an end to my hypocrisy?" he asked his saintly guest.

The rebbe replied in his trademark singsong, "You may be insincere in your giving, but the poor people you feed are very sincerely satiated."

7. Should My Gift Be Publicized?

PUBLICITY

Humility and selflessness are intertwined with sanctity and virtue. Conversely, Judaism sees ego and arrogance as particularly repugnant. We are encouraged to shun publicity and perform deeds of righteousness and kindness as discreetly as possible. Indeed, Jewish lore is replete with tales of hidden saints and discreet benefactors, and it roundly condemns egos that swell in proportion to burgeoning wallets. After all, we aspire to serve God, not our egos.

Astonishingly, this same tradition encourages publicizing the identities of notable donors to charitable causes (when there is no concern that this will shame a recipient). The Torah does so itself, and Jewish law applauds this as a means of inspiring others to perform charitable acts. While modesty is certainly a personal ideal that refines a donor's character and safeguards his or her altruism, this is far outweighed by the benefit to the Jewish collective caused by outpourings of generosity from the many who are touched and moved to action as a result of a publicized gift to a worthy cause.

Modesty may make a better individual, but acclaimed contributions create a better world. Therefore eschewing anonymity is itself a tangible act of charity—an act that persists long after the initial deed.

Moreover, because the Torah encourages us to serve as role models, it thereby paves the ethically fragile path of publicity with Divine reinforcement. If we act publicly for God's sake, God assumes responsibility for protecting us from any adverse impact to our characters. We must select the path of greatest good, and trust in our Creator to crown our efforts with optimal success.

Sources: Micah 6:8; Talmud, Avodah Zarah 18b; Proverbs 21:14 with Rashi, ad loc.; Talmud, Bava Batra 9b–10a; Ketubot 67b; Rabbi Shlomo Ben Aderet, *Responsa* 1:581; Ruth 2:14; Midrash, *Ruth Rabah* 5:6; Genesis 37:21; *Responsa Divrei Malkiel*, Introduction; *Teshuvot Vehanhagot* 2:481.

Certificate for a donation made to an old age home in Jerusalem, Vilna, 1913. (YIVO Institute for Jewish Research, New York)

SUPPORTING TEXTS

BIBLICAL PRECEDENTS FOR PUBLICIZING THE IDENTITY OF SPONSORS
Rabbi Shlomo Ben Aderet, *Responsa* **1:581**

Question: Reuben had a home near the synagogue . . . and he wanted to connect it to the the synagogue in order to enlarge the synagogue. . . . Reuben wanted to have his name written over the entranceway so that he would be remembered for his donation, but a few members of the congregation objected. . . .

Response: I do not see that the congregation can refuse him, neither by law nor on the basis of proper behavior. Who could stop someone from memorializing his name on a building that he pledged? No one can restrict others from doing as they please with their donations. Moreover, such written dedications are the accepted custom in several holy congregations, and in our own locale, such a dedication is written on the wall of the synagogue. This is the way of the pious and veteran sages—to provide a reward for doing a mitzvah.

In fact, this is the way of the Torah as well—to record and publicize one who does a mitzvah. For when Reuben saved Joseph from his brothers, Scripture writes afterward (Genesis 37:21), "Reuben heard and saved Joseph from their hand." So, too, when Boaz gave bread and vinegar to Ruth, Scripture recorded it (Ruth 2:14). Indeed, many acts of benevolence are lauded in the writings of the prophets. If the Torah does so, then we should follow its path, inasmuch as all of its paths are paths of pleasantness.

ENCOURAGING OTHERS TO DONATE
Rabbi Malkiel Tenenbaum, *Responsa Divrei Malkiel,* **Introduction**

Rabbi Shlomo ben Aderet wrote that those who donate can publicize their good deed. But this is difficult to understand because . . . all *mitzvot* are to be performed with a spirit of modesty, so that arrogance does not infiltrate one's mind. . . .

The explanation is as follows: There is a well-known aphorism of our sages (*Ethics of the Fathers* 4:17) that "one hour of repentance and good deeds in this world is greater than all of the World to Come." How can we continue to perform good deeds in this world even after death? This can be accomplished when a mitzvah becomes synonymous with our name. . . . In fact, when we are publicly identified as a proponent of a mitzvah, others will follow and their observance will be attributed to our influence. . . . Thus, it would seem that the reason why it is preferable to publicize *mitzvot* is so that others will emulate the positive behavior. Those passages that encourage modesty refer to *mitzvot* that are known to all and that everyone performs; thus, publicizing their performance adds nothing. But we should publicize those who perform *mitzvot* that lie insufficiently observed, so that others will follow.

DEPENDS ON THE RECIPIENT
Rabbi Moshe Sternbuch, *Teshuvot Vehanhagot* 2:481

We must distinguish between providing for the poor and donating to Jewish institutions. When giving to the poor, it should be done discreetly, because publicity can be detrimental to them. But when giving to an institution, it is appropriate to publicize the gift, so that others are inspired to emulate this behavior.

STORY Approximately three thousand years ago, the ancient kingdom of Israel was visited by a righteous Moabite convert called Ruth. She arrived as the Jewish farmers began their annual barley harvest. Not having any food or the ability to establish a means of supporting herself, she took advantage of the Torah's stipulations that ensure that certain parts of every harvest are left for the needy to collect.

She found herself gathering overlooked stalks of grain in the field of Boaz, a distinguished and righteous leader from the tribe of Judah. When Boaz entered his field to oversee the harvesting process, he noticed Ruth's extraordinary modesty and her attention to the precise details of the Torah's laws governing the agricultural gifts to the poor. At lunchtime, he offered her the opportunity to join the reapers in their meal, and he handed her some parched barley to eat.

He eventually married Ruth and their great-grandson was none other than the righteous King David, who changed the course of Jewish history. It all began with an act of caring for a hungry pauper that was later recorded for posterity in the Book of Ruth.

Our sages, however, offer an interesting observation (Midrash, *Ruth Rabah* 5:6). They note that Boaz offered Ruth a modest meal—the amount of parched grain that could be held in one hand. Had he known that his deed would be recorded in the Torah for all times, our sages insist, he would have fed her a royal feast of fattened calves.

Our sages thereby inform us that despite Boaz's saintliness and charity, he would have been inspired to do far more had he realized that he was in the public spotlight. This serves to underscore the tremendous benefits of giving charitably before the eyes of the public.

8. A History of Jewish Giving

HISTORY

Some might expect that a people repeatedly uprooted and pillaged would become hardened. The Jews, however, never abandoned their sensitivity, nor their hallmark generosity. Historical records from each era demonstrate astonishing communal and individual commitment to charity as a way of life.

Maimonides, for example, lived in twelfth-century Spain, Morocco, the Holy Land, and finally Egypt. He corresponded frequently with Jewish communities across the globe, who sent representatives to consult with him. He testified that "we have never seen nor heard of a Jewish community that does not have a charity fund,"[1] and that the funds were collected from each individual.

Similarly, records show that the practice of calculating one-tenth of all earnings and donating that amount to charity has been practiced by Jews throughout history and was a standard factor when making financial calculations. So, for example, a monetary commitment might be enlarged by one-tenth to enable the recipient himself to also donate the customary tenth to charity, while retaining the originally intended sum.

---

1. *Mishneh Torah,* Laws of Gifts to the Poor 9:1–3.

The pervasiveness and consistency of Jewish philanthropy has amazed outside observers to this day. Jews remain disproportionately generous, regularly topping the philanthropic charts, even in societies that are very charitable. Perhaps more importantly, Jews of lesser means give more charity than their fellow citizens in similar economic circumstances. They give even when there isn't a societal expectation to be a philanthropist, because giving is embedded in the Jewish conscience. We remain forever a charitable wonder to the nations.

Sources: *Tsava'ot Yehudah ben HaRosh Ve'achiv Yaakov* (Pressburg 1845), pp. 15–16; *Maaser Kesafim* (Jerusalem, 1977), p. 48; *The Downing Street Years* (New York: HarperCollins, 1993), p. 509; "Jews Take 5 of Top 6 Spots in Annual List of Top U.S. Givers," *Jewish Telegraphic Agency,* February 8, 2011.

Jews receiving matzah for Passover. Brzesc nad Bugiem (Brest-on-the-Bug [River], Belarus/Poland border), 1921. (YIVO Institute for Jewish Research, New York)

SUPPORTING TEXTS

EVERY COMMUNITY HAD A FUND, EVERY JEW DONATED

Maimonides, *Mishneh Torah*, Laws of Gifts to the Poor 9:1–3

In every city where Jews live, they are obligated to appoint trustworthy, well-known individuals as trustees of a charitable fund. They should circulate among the people every Friday and collect funds, based on their assessment of what each person is able to give. . . .

We have never seen nor heard of a Jewish community that does not have a charity fund.

A TENTH OF ALL EARNINGS—1314

Rabbi Asher ben Yechiel (Rosh), cited by his son Rabbi Yehudah in his ethical will, *Tsava'ot Yehudah ben HaRosh Ve'achiv Yaakov* (Pressburg, 1845), pp. 15–16

"Listen, my child, to your father's instruction, and do not forsake your mother's teaching" (Proverbs 1:8). In the city [of Cologne] from which we emigrated, our ancestors for many generations gave away a tenth of all their income to *tzedakah*, for various mitzvah purposes. This was rooted in our sages' statement on the verse, "You shall tithe *all* the crop," namely, that the Torah intends to include the income of those who do not work in agriculture but travel for business instead—they ought to give away a tenth for Torah causes.

We have therefore committed to follow the path of our ancestors, and we have taken upon ourselves to tithe all of our profits, whether they be from sales or interest. . . . We have accepted upon ourselves and our children to be careful about this practice. . . . Today, the ninth of Cheshvan 5075 (October, 1314). Signed by Rabbi Asher ben Yechiel and his four sons.

A TENTH OF ALL EARNINGS—1730

Dowry arrangement, from the year 1730, cited in *Maaser Kesafim* (Jerusalem, 1977), p. 48

Mazal Tov! . . . These are the conditions and commitments that were discussed and agreed upon by the two sides: Shimon Wolf Wertheim representing his son Shmuel, the groom, and Isaac Oppenheim, representing his daughter, Sarah, the bride.

Wolf commits for this son's dowry 27,500 Rhenish gold, so that after his son deducts *maaser* (one-tenth), the total will be the handsome sum of 25,000 Rhenish gold in cash. Isaac commits for his daughter's dowry 33,000 Rhenish gold, which means that after she gives *maaser*, the total will be the handsome sum of 30,000 Rhenish gold. . . .

JEWISH COMMUNITIES CARED FOR ALL THEIR MEMBERS

Prime Minister Margaret Thatcher, *The Downing Street Years* (New York: HarperCollins, 1993), p. 509

I have enormous admiration for the Jewish people. . . . My old constituency of Finchley has a large Jewish population. In the thirty-three years I represented it I never had a Jew come in poverty and desperation to one of my constituency surgeries. They had always been looked after by their own.

TODAY'S JEWS REMAIN DISPROPORTIONATELY CHARITABLE

Jewish Telegraphic Agency, **February 8, 2011**

In 2010, the top philanthropists in the United States contributed approximately $3.3 billion to charity, according to the *Chronicle's* Philanthropy 50, a list that tracks the largest gifts made by individuals each year....

At least 19 of the 53 individuals and couples named on the list are Jewish, including five of the list's top six....

Jews traditionally rank high on such lists and figure prominently among the country's elite philanthropists. Jews also make up more than half of the first 57 billionaires to join the Bill Gates and Warren Buffet Giving Pledge—a group of ultra-wealthy Americans who have pledged to give away more than half of their assets during their lifetime.

LOWER-INCOME JEWS MORE LIKELY TO GIVE

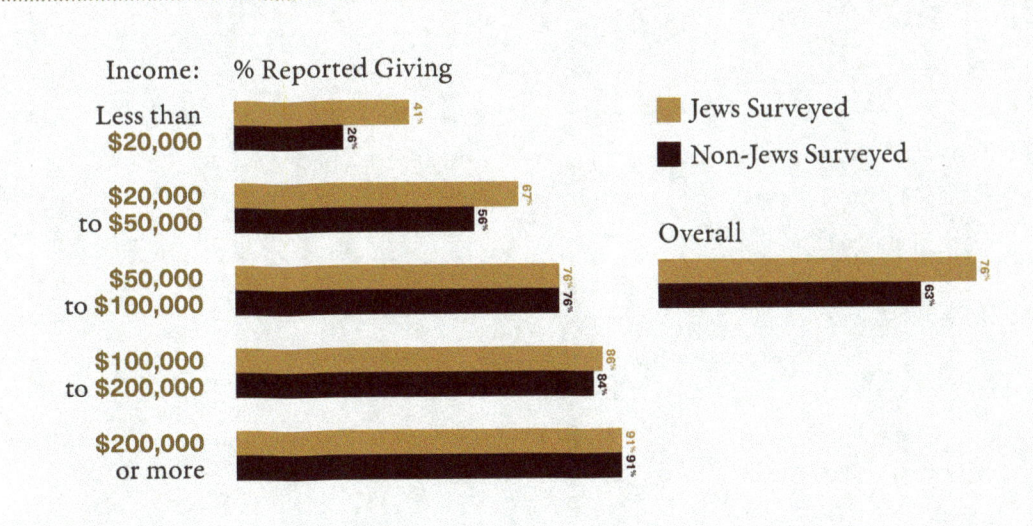

Income: % Reported Giving

- Less than $20,000: Jews 41%, Non-Jews 26%
- $20,000 to $50,000: Jews 67%, Non-Jews 56%
- $50,000 to $100,000: Jews 76%, Non-Jews 76%
- $100,000 to $200,000: Jews 86%, Non-Jews 84%
- $200,000 or more: Jews 91%, Non-Jews 91%

Overall: Jews 76%, Non-Jews 63%

■ Jews Surveyed
■ Non-Jews Surveyed

Source: Connected to Give: National Study of American Jewish Giving, Key Findings (2013)

9. Instilling the Value of *Tzedakah*

INSTILLING THE VALUE

The first Jew in history may have also been the most charitable. But God did not love Abraham for his extreme generosity as much as He loved him for dedicating his time and effort to raising future generations of givers.

It requires time and effort to achieve this quintessential Jewish goal. Had Abraham simply given Isaac inspiring talks about the importance of charity, he would not have guaranteed that his descendants would consider *tzedakah* central to their way of life. Instead, Abraham set a personal example, from serving guests to ceremoniously donating a tenth of all his earnings (*maaser*). So well did he model his attitude toward charitable activities that he inspired all subsequent generations of Jews to serve as charitable role models to their own children.

Nowadays, our youth require more than the personal examples set by their elders—although those are absolutely critical. It is necessary to draw them into a charitable life through creative hands-on projects. We must seek ways to provide them with opportunities to experience the satisfaction and goodness of giving, on a regular basis.

This begins at home, by training them to calculate a tenth of monies they receive and to donate it to *tzedakah*, and continues with communal projects. For best results, *tzedakah* projects should be placed into their hands, so that their sense of responsibility ensures that the trait of charity becomes their own—to the point that they will be inspired to raise their own children in the same caring path.

Sources: Genesis 18:19; *Ketav Sofer,* ad loc.; *Likutei Sichot* 16:625; "Role-Modeling and Conversations About Giving in the Socialization of Adolescent Charitable Giving and Volunteering," *Journal of Adolescence* 37:1 (January 2014), p. 53.

Charity box, unknown artist, brass, Persia, c. 19th century. (Minneapolis Institute of Art)

SUPPORTING TEXTS

CONVINCE THE NEXT GENERATION

Rabbi Avraham Shmuel Binyamin Sofer, *Ketav Sofer,* ad loc.

"I love Abraham because he instructs his children and his household after him that they should keep the way of God by performing *tzedakah* and justice" (Genesis 18:19). The education Abraham imparted was such that even "*after him,*" when he was no longer around to instruct his offspring, they were guaranteed to "keep the way of God by performing *tzedakah* and justice." They did so, not in deference to their father Abraham's wishes, but because they understood that it was the right and just thing to do.

***TZEDAKAH* PROJECTS BY SCHOOL STUDENTS**

The Lubavitcher Rebbe, *Likutei Sichot* 16:625

It is very appropriate and worthwhile for school principals and teachers . . . to recommend and encourage their students, boys and girls, including and especially those who have not yet reached the age of bar or bat mitzvah, to increase . . . their charitable activities. Namely, the students of each school (or each class) should establish a free-loan fund . . . and from time to time, each student should contribute some of his or her own money to this fund. . . .

In order to instill in the students' hearts the importance of personal charitable involvement and volunteer work—in addition to monetary generosity—it is most proper that these free-loan funds be directed by the boys and girls themselves, with the students of the school (or the class) choosing from among themselves a director, a treasurer, etc. The fact that this fund is being administered by the students' representatives will cause them to have a stronger feeling of responsibility and personal commitment to the cause (which will, in turn, increase their energy and enthusiasm as well).

It would be best to alternate from time to time (by way of student vote) the directorship of the free-loan fund as well as its various management positions (director, treasurer, bookkeeper, etc.), in order to enable all the students, or at the least a majority, to be (not just donors of money but also) donors of their time and energy.

ENCOURAGING CHILDREN VIA THEIR PARENTS

Mark Ottoni-Wilhelm, et al., "Role-Modeling and Conversations about Giving in the Socialization of Adolescent Charitable Giving and Volunteering," *Journal of Adolescence* 37:1 (January 2014), p. 53

This study investigated the relationship between the monetary giving and volunteering behavior of adolescents and the role-modeling and conversations about giving provided by their parents. The participants are a large nationally-representative sample of 12–18-year-olds. . . . Adolescents reported whether they gave money and whether they volunteered. In a separate interview parents reported whether they talked to their adolescents' about giving. In a third interview, parents reported whether they gave money and volunteered. The results show that both role-modeling and conversations about giving are strongly related to adolescents' giving and volunteering. Knowing that both role-modeling and conversation are strongly related to adolescents' giving and volunteering suggests an often overlooked way for practitioners and policy-makers to nurture giving and volunteering among adults: start earlier, during adolescence, by guiding parents in their role-modeling of, and conversations about, charitable giving and volunteering.

INCREASED PROBABILITY ADOLESCENTS WILL GIVE WHEN PARENTS...

Converse about giving	+11%
Role-model giving	+15%

Source: Mark Ottoni-Wilhelm, et al., 2014, ibid.

The Rabbi's Cheder Test, *Nandor Vydai Brenner (1903-1944), Hungary, oil on canvas.*

Instilling the value of charitable giving generates a lasting positive impact on future generations.

This dynamic is aptly demonstrated in statements issued by prominent Jewish philanthropists, each of whom attributes much of their own attitude toward philanthropy to having been raised with the value of *tzedakah*.

"My parents instilled in me Jewish values and ethics that I have carried with me throughout my life, and which have guided every aspect of my work in business, government, and philanthropy."

Michael R. Bloomberg

"Philanthropy is in the DNA of my family. My parents were both active participants in Jewish, local Montreal and Canadian charities. The dining table conversation was a place for discussing what was important to them in that world. . . . It is no surprise then, that each of us has contributed to society."

Charles R. Bronfman

"One of my parents would give me a dime and say, 'Go to Sunday school and give it away.' I'd think, 'I have to give this dime away?' It was hurting me. And they said, 'There are people who need it more than you, so just do it.' But I did it reluctantly, and I was a little crabby about it. I had to grow into the knowledge of what that was. I thought that if I gave it away I'd be losing something, and that's what I learned later on—that you get it back."

Nancy Grand

"Joan and I recall growing up in homes that honored the Jewish obligation of *tzedakah* by frequently placing coins in a small box (*pushke*).... Societal needs as recognized by *tzedakah* are part of our inheritance."

Joan and Irwin Jacobs

"Growing up in a small apartment, we didn't have much. And yet throughout the week, my family put pennies away into a little blue box. Seeing this I understood: even when it seems like we have nothing, we nevertheless continue to give. No matter our differences, we are one people, and we have a responsibility for each other."

Mike Leven

"*Tzedakah* is part of our livelihood. It is how I grew up—with *tzedakah* in my household."

Bernard Marcus

"We both have strong ties to our Jewish heritage, and charitable giving, also known as *tzedakah*, is a cornerstone of our culture and upbringing. We are committed to promoting a strong Jewish culture in our community, promoting tolerance and understanding among different religious cultures, and supporting the State of Israel."

Henry and Susan Samueli

From a Jewish perspective, what matters most is not the amount of a donation, but the effort and dedication involved—are we giving what we are truly able to give?—in light of individual circumstances and ability.

Vintage Jewish New Year's greeting card (detail) depicting the practice of giving extra charity during the auspicious month of Tishrei.

STORY Rabbi Shne'ur Zalman of Liadi (1745–1812) was raising funds to ransom Jewish prisoners. Upon his arrival at a certain town, the community elders received him graciously and agreed to accompany him to the homes of potential donors. At the same time, they warned him not to visit the town's infamous miser. It simply wasn't worth it. The miser would respond to every request for charity by offering a single rusty coin, which even the most desperate pauper would promptly refuse. Rabbi Shne'ur Zalman, however, insisted on visiting the miser. After providing the gentleman a brief description of the cause, the miser proceed to offer the rabbi a single rusty coin. To the miser's surprise, Rabbi Shne'ur Zalman seemed delighted with the gift. He offered the miser a grateful smile as he slipped the rusty coin into his pocket. "Thank you!" he exclaimed, "May God bless and protect you!"

As the rabbi left the residence, one of the elders who accompanied him hissed, "You should have thrown it back in his face!" Rabbi Shne'ur Zalman did not respond.

All of a sudden, they heard the door reopening behind them. The miser called out, "Rabbis! Wait! Please come back." They dutifully returned and were shocked when the miser asked, "How much money do you need to ransom these prisoners?"

"Five thousand rubles," replied Rabbi Shne'ur Zalman. The miser reached into his purse and handed him one thousand. "Thank you! Thank you!" gushed Rabbi Shne'ur Zalman, warmly blessing the man before leaving the home.

Before they could get far, the rich man came running after them. "I changed my mind," he panted. "I have decided to give the entire sum needed for the ransom."

"What is the meaning of this?" the astonished elders asked their esteemed guest after leaving the rich man's home with the full sum. "How did you get that notorious miser to give five thousand rubles?"

"This man is no miser," Rabbi Shne'ur Zalman responded. "No Jewish soul truly is. But how could he give if he never experienced the joy of giving? Every time he offered his rusty penny, the recipient rejected it. All he needed was to taste the satisfaction of a successful donation."

*Charity box, unknown artist, Israel, c. 1920.
(Minneapolis Institute of Art)*

10. The Time Is Now

THE TIME

Anyone familiar with Jewish law and ritual is aware that it is keen on fine details. Each mitzvah includes specifications so that it will be accomplished correctly. It may therefore come as a surprise that the Torah strongly *discourages* delaying the fulfillment of God's will for the sake of perfecting the act. "If not now, when?" urge the ancient sages.[1] Immediacy is paramount.

God cherished Abraham for his speed in fulfilling the most difficult commands. Abraham rushed to lovingly sacrifice not merely the mandatory tenth of earnings, or much of his great wealth, but even his precious son, as God had instructed. No blood was shed in the end, but God recorded Abraham's alacrity as an eternal lesson for the Jewish people.

Nowhere is immediacy more critical than in the mitzvah of *tzedakah*. There are countless causes, Torah institutions, and champions of Jewish continuity. It is natural to ensure effective spending by thoroughly vetting recipients before offering sizable donations. That is the logical approach, but, in an era of unprecedented challenges that face the Jewish people, many Jewish organizations are like firefighters battling residential wildfires.

---

1. *Ethics of the Fathers* 1:14.

Immediacy trumps perfection when the continuity of so many is at risk.

More personally, it is our duty to seize the earliest opportunities to give *tzedakah* and to complete the donation as swiftly as possible. This is most beneficial for recipients, and also for donors, in securing their daily blessings from God.

Sources: *Igeret Hakodesh* 11; *Menorat Hama'or, Ner Hashelishi, Kelal* 7, 2:10; The Lubavitcher Rebbe, English letter to Mr. I. I. Stone, July 30, 1973; Rabbi David ibn Zimra, *Responsa* 4:13.

Donation coupon for Keren Ha'yishuv, a fund dedicated to strengthening Orthodox life in the Land of Israel. Warsaw, 1935. (YIVO Institute for Jewish Research, New York)

SUPPORTING TEXTS

ACT WITH URGENCY
Mishnah, *Ethics of the Fathers* 1:14

Hillel said: "If I am not for myself, who will be for me? But if I am only for myself, what am I? And if not now, when?"

DISREGARD DOUBTS
Rabbi Yitschak Abuhav, *Menorat Hama'or, Ner Hashelishi, Kelal 7*, 2:10

Do not withhold from giving *tzedakah* to anyone who asks. It is better to give to one who does not really need it, than to refrain from giving to those who truly are in need.

EXCESSIVE RESEARCH CAUSES DELAY AND DAMAGE
The Lubavitcher Rebbe, English letter to Mr. I. I. Stone, The Jacob Saperstein Foundation, July 30, 1973

It has often happened, unfortunately, in various areas of philanthropy, that before actual distribution of funds is commenced, a preliminary and lengthy research or study program is initiated. While this approach is generally motivated by a desire to distribute funds more effectively, and may be commendable theoretically, the net result has all too often been to delay actual distribution of funds [that are] urgently needed, immediately, quite apart from the fact that substantial funds have thus been diverted from their main purpose....

A further point, which is also mentioned in your letter, is the prevalent policy of foundations not to touch the principal at any time, but to make distributions from income only. This policy, too, may be commendable in normal times, but in times of emergency such as now exist, I believe that a more flexible policy is clearly called for. Obviously, however substantial the income may be, it is only a fraction of the actual reserve; and where there is a case of life-saving, some of the reserves should also be brought into play.

I repeat, I fully appreciate that both guiding principles mentioned above, with which I take issue, are unquestionably businesslike and well-intentioned. But they are sound only in normal times.

The reality of the situation is, however, that we live in abnormal times.... We see to our deep sorrow and dismay how a large and growing segment of our Jewish youth is utterly confused and alienated.... Fortunately ... the negative side of the situation is compensated by the positive side of it. It is, that never before has there been a greater, more eager and honest desire on the part of our young generation to search for the truth.... The combination of the said two factors, the negative and the positive, makes it even more compelling to render the needed help immediately, without delay and in the maximum measure.

SEIZE THE FIRST OPPORTUNITY
Rabbi David ibn Zimra, *Responsa* 4:13

Question: Reuben is incarcerated and thus precluded from praying in a synagogue and performing various *mitzvot*. Despite his entreaties to the governor, permission was only granted for him to leave prison one day a year—whichever day Reuben chooses. May our teacher instruct us regarding which day Reuben should choose to go to the synagogue?

Response: I have seen a contemporary sage who responded to this question, but he sank like lead in raging waters, came up with nothing more than shards, and built his arguments on a faulty foundation. At first, he wrote that Yom Kippur is preferable. Then, he shifted to say that Purim would be preferable—so that this Jew could hear the Scroll of Esther with a quorum and in a highly publicized manner.

Do not rely on this. It would be more appropriate to rely on the Talmudic law (Pesachim 64b), "We do not pass over a mitzvah opportunity," a unanimously held halachic precept. Therefore, precedence should be given to the very first occasion upon which there is an opportunity to perform a mitzvah that cannot be performed in prison. It is irrelevant whether it is a weighty mitzvah or a light one, [as *Ethics of the Fathers* 2:1 says, "Be careful with a minor mitzvah as with a major one, for] we do not know the reward of the *mitzvot*." To me, this ruling is patently obvious.

Tzedakah *boxes for various charities.*